Sum

of

Educated

Tara Westover

Conversation Starters

By BookHabits

Tips for Using BookHabits Conversation Starters:

EVERY GOOD BOOK CONTAINS A WORLD FAR DEEPER THAN the surface of its pages. The characters and their world come alive through the words on the pages, yet the characters and its world still live on. Questions herein are designed to bring us beneath the surface of the page and invite us into the world that lives on. These questions can be used to:

- Foster a deeper understanding of the book
- Promote an atmosphere of discussion for groups
- Assist in the study of the book, either individually or corporately
- Explore unseen realms of the book as never seen before

About Us:

THROUGH YEARS OF EXPERIENCE AND FIELD EXPERTISE, from newspaper featured book clubs to local library chapters, *BookHabits* can bring your book discussion to life. Host your book party as we discuss some of today's most widely read books.

Table of Contents

Introducing *Educated*

"EDUCATED" IS TARA WESTOVER'S MEMOIR THAT takes readers through her journey to define who she is and the sort of life she wanted for herself—a difficult task considering her beginnings. Westover was born into a fundamentalist Mormon family. Her parents were survivalists that believed the end of the world was coming and they needed to prepare their seven children for that inevitability. When he was 30, her father started believing his children were in danger of the influence of the Illuminati. He pulled them out of school. The four other children that he would later have (Westover being the youngest of them all) would not have any formal education or even a birth certificate.

As suggested by its title, "Educated" came from Westover's self-reflection on her education. It's what fundamentally made her upbringing so different, what created such a gap between her and the peers she came to know when she first set foot in a classroom at the age of 17. It was the fact that her educational system had been so stark in contrast to theirs. Her earliest educational experiences consisted of helping her mother with her herbalist medicine and midwifery. Once she got older, her education consisted of the hard labor of working in her father's junkyard alongside him and her siblings. The work was brutal and dangerous. It was a situation that violated nearly every law the Occupational Safety and Health Administration stood for. Fingers were lost, concussions were endured, and terrifying burn marks were sustained. Not believing in modern medicine, her father and mother treated all of these with herbs and naturalistic practices. These injuries were made worse by the fact that her father was prone to violence and had tendencies reflective of someone with bipolar disorder. He would throw large pieces of scrap metal at her and her siblings without any second thought. She had an older brother who was naturally prone to violent tendencies—possibly the result of such a violent father—but whom became more violent after a blow to the head by a rebar.

She only learned of a world different from the one she knew because of another one of her older brothers' choice to leave for school. He studied secretly, went to college at Brigham Young University, and came back with tales of what it was like outside the world that their parents had created. Westover was fascinated and wanted to follow in her brother's footsteps. She studied what she could from the limited resources available to her—religious and devotional literature mostly— and obtained the information she needed to take the ACT. She got into Brigham Young University and her life changed forever. She learned about things she had never heard of before like the Holocaust and other monumental events of the world that we all take as everyday knowledge. She was captivated by this whole new world and continued in her search of it as she became a fellow at Harvard and obtained her PhD from Cambridge. She studied history and philosophy.

The violence from the males she in her family that she had experienced in her early life was a natural thing that she accepted. She recalls an experience when she came home during a break from Cambridge. Though she had been learning about the teachings of feminism and had accepted them as valuable thoughts she wanted to take on as her own, she still sat quietly as she watched her brother abuse his wife. She explains that though she had accepted the teaching that women are human beings who have the same rights and should be treated equally to men, her body had not obeyed the thoughts her mind had accepted as truth as she kept silent. This theme follows throughout "Educated." She struggles between the life she knew and the new world she was taking in. She struggles to find the balance that each of us have when we fly from the nest, so to speak. Her struggle just happens to be one that stems for a seemingly deeply unique situation. The dilemma she puts forth is what do we take with us when we leave home and what's best to leave behind. She does so in a captivating way and style that mimics short story formatting.

"Educated" is a New York Times Bestseller that has captured the fascination of the public. Its New York Times Book Review marked it as so captivating and shocking that it's the sort of prose that could "tranquilize elephants." It received a high ranking on Amazon's best sellers as number 80 out of 100 and it received a 4.5 star review on the website.

Discussion Questions

"Get Ready to Enter a New World"

Tip: Begin with questions dealing with broader issues to ensure ample time for quality discussions. Read through all discussion questions before engaging.

~ ~ ~

question 1

Westover discusses her internal struggle between wanting to know life outside her family and wanting to remain loyal to her familial ties. Why do you think she holds so tightly to her family when they have kept so much from her?

~ ~ ~

~~~

question 2

Westover suffered abuse from both her father and her brother and yet she remained with them. Why do you think the thought to run away was never an option she considered?

~~~

question 3

Throughout her memoir, Westover discusses the pull she feels toward her family, no matter how much of what the taught her is discredited in her experience in the real world. Why do you think she feels such a pull even still?

~~~

question 4

There is a theme of home found throughout "Educated." How does Westover explore this term? What do you think her definition of it is? What's yours?

~~~

~ ~ ~

question 5

There is an incident in Westover's memoir where she discusses how embedded the patriarchy is in her subconscious. Even as she studies and accepts feminism, she struggles in contradicting the patriarchy that still held in her family. How do you think this reflects the relationship between our foundational understanding of social ecosystems and what we come to learn for ourselves? Does it say anything about patriarchy/feminism?

~ ~ ~

question 6

Westover was very limited in her study resources. What sort of skill do you think it took for her to prepare herself for the ACTs as well as the world at large?

~~~

question 7

Westover was raised in a fundamentalist Mormon home—a radical break off group of the LDS church—yet she chose to attend Brigham Young University (BYU). BYU is a school that's sponsored by the LDS church. Do you think there was a conscious correlation in choosing this university? What does it say about her ties to her educational foundation?

~~~

~~~

question 8

Westover discusses how when she first went off on her own she thought she would go and get a degree, get married, and then move back to the life she knew. However, that never happened. Why do you think that is? Do you think it was a conscious rebellion or just something that happened naturally?

~~~

~~~

question 9

Westover remains in contact with some of the people she grew up with. They even helped her write "Educated." Why do you think she remains in contact with them even though there's such a stark contrast in their lifestyles?

~~~

~~~

question 10

Westover's father was rather violent toward her and experienced extreme paranoia. How do you think this affected her learning? Did it make her skeptical? Did such violence deter her from accepting anything she was ever taught?

~~~

question 11

Westover was no stranger to the extremes of life even before she left home. She helped her mother with midwifery, experienced abuse from a brother and her father, and saw several of her siblings lose fingers and sustain serious injuries because of their junkyard work. Do you think this prepared her for the intensities she would have to face in the outside world?

question 12

Westover chose the title of "Educated" for a reason. In your opinion, what do you think that reason is? What does it mean to her to be educated or have an education?

~~~

question 13

Westover endured an extreme beginning. Do you think this would lead her to an extreme life on the opposite side of the spectrum she had been taught from?

~~~

~~~

question 14

The only exposure Westover had to history came from religious and devotional literature. It wasn't until she was in a university class that she learned what the Holocaust was. Do you think such a warped view of history caused her to obtain her PhD in history? Do you think the same could be said of her master's in Philosophy?

~~~

question 15

Despite the fact that they lived in such extreme conditions, Westover clearly looked to her siblings, especially her university-educated brother, for guidance. Do you think this is what still holds her pull toward them?

~ ~ ~

question 16

"Educated" has seen raving reviews from highly acclaimed sources, such as the New York Times. What makes Westover's story so fascinating for everyone? Is it how different her background is or how fundamentally similar it is to everyone else's who leaves home?

~ ~ ~

question 17

Westover came from an extreme break off group known as Mormon fundamentalists. Why do you think the world is so fascinated by groups such as this?

~~~

question 18

Westover clearly valued her education, spending a decade catching up with several degrees and creating a memoir inspired by the very idea of what an education is. How important is education to functioning in society?

~~~

~~~

question 19

Westover wrote in a style akin to short stories. She was inspired by the fascination she gained from reading short stories during her time of writing her memoir. How do you think this style contributes to her connecting to her readers? How do you think it hinders that relationship?

~~~

~~~

question 20

Nearly all the reviews of "Educated" point out that Westover was 17 when she entered her first formal classroom. Why is this so shocking considering it's the case for several others who were homeschooled?

~~~

Introducing the Author

TARA WESTOVER WAS BORN IN IDAHO. SHE GREW UP in a small community, the population of which was less than 300. Her parents were fundamental Mormon survivalists that taught their children a homeschooled curriculum based on the reading of religious and devotional literature and engaging in activities that would help them to learn the necessary survival skills they would need for the end of the world. Their isolated unit focused on an education that included herbal medicines—as her father did not trust doctors or schools that were so-called "controlled" by the government—

administered by Westover's mother. Her parents were firm believers that no one could teach you anything better than you could teach it to yourself.

Growing up, Westover would help her mother with her midwifery and herbal medicine. She did so until she was old enough to help her father with his business of scrapping metal in his junkyard and building barns and hay sheds in the community. The physical danger of such intense labor was elevated by the fact that her father was rather hot tempered. This meant she endured several violent attacks of him hitting her with scrap metal. The violence did not end with her father, however. After a rebar accident that gave him a nasty head injury, one of her older brothers who was already violent in his tendencies became even more so and she often fell victim to his rage.

The youngest of seven children, Tara was blind to anything and everything outside of her small community until one of her older brothers decided to rebel. He studied in secret, got into college, and left his isolated world. He returned to his family and told Tara of the outside world. This sparked inspiration inside her to follow in his footsteps and gain a proper education. She too studied in secret so that she would be able to gain the necessary knowledge she needed to get a good score on the ACT that would get her into a university. She set foot in a formal classroom for the first time when she was 17. She attended Brigham Young

University where she pursued her bachelor's degree. After graduating, she became a visiting fellow at Harvard University and then attended Cambridge to earn her PhD in history.

Westover now lives in a flat in London. It was here, after she obtained her PhD, that she decided to write "Educated." She gained help from friends and family she was still in touch with from her early years and a writing group in London that gave their brutal and honest opinions. It was they who exposed her to the idea of writing her narrative in a sort of short story format. Having no idea what a short story was, she decided the only way to learn how to do it and what it was was to expose herself to any and every short story she could get her hands on. She found her style and voice in these stories, which enabled her to tell her story in a way that she felt comfortable. This is how she formed her voice that can be found in "Educated."

Fireside Questions

"What would you do?"

Tip: These questions can be a fun exercise as it spurs creativity among the readers by allowing alternate scene endings and "if this was you" questions.

~~~

question 21

Rather than fearing the outside world, Westover was fascinated by it, even though she had been told nothing but paranoia and isolation. Why do you think made her more curious than fearful of the unknown?

~~~

~~~

question 22

Westover gained philosophy and history degrees. Why do you think she chose these particular fields?

~~~

~~~

question 23

While Westover grew up in an isolated mountainside in Idaho, she settled in a flat in London. Why do you think she chose such a stark contrast to settle into in her adult life?

~~~

~~~

question 24

Westover was inspired by her older brother's decision to study in secret and go off to college. If it wasn't for him, do you think she would have done the same?

~~~

question 25

Westover's father did not trust doctors, so her mother practiced herbal medicine on their children even with extreme injuries like lost fingers and concussions. Though Westover came to trust doctors on her own, do you think such an extreme naturalistic upbringing would have made her distrust naturalistic medicine?

~ ~ ~

question 26

Westover spent the first 17 years of her life living in an isolated community. Do you think you would have survived living in such an intensely remote environment?

~ ~ ~

~~~

question 27

Rather than being fearful when her brother told her about a world outside their community, Westover became intrigued and wanted to learn more. Do you think you would have been curious like her or fearful like her father?

~~~

~~~

question 28

Westover didn't know about important historical events or figures when she first began her education. She had to ask a professor at her university what the Holocaust was. Do you think you would have found such a gap in your knowledge overwhelming or encouraging if you were in her shoes?

~~~

~~~

question 29

Westover's professors were shocked and fascinated by the fact that she didn't know about famous events in history, but they encouraged and supported her nonetheless. If you were in their shoes, do you think you would have been supportive of feeding her appetite to learn or would you have shrunk from the opportunity to feed such a hungry mind that was lacking so much basic knowledge?

~~~

question 30

There was one incident in Westover's life where she experienced tonsillitis and her father told her to open her mouth to the sun to let it heal. She did so for days. Do you think you would have endured such extreme measures of health treatment?

Quiz Questions

"Ready to Announce the Winners?"

Tip: Create a leaderboard and track scores to see who gets the most correct answers. Winners required. Prizes optional.

~~~

quiz question 1

True or False: "Educated" explores what the title's word actually means. Westover does not value formal education, but values her homeschooled education more.

~~~

quiz question 2

True or False: Westover was inspired by one of her siblings to get a formal education. This was on older brother.

quiz question 3

In her early life, Westover helped her mother with her job. She worked in herbal medicine and
_____.

quiz question 4

Westover came from a large family. She had
_____ siblings.

quiz question 5

Westover gained several degrees. They were degrees in the subjects of philosophy and _____.

quiz question 6

Once she was old enough, she learned to help her father in his business. This was a _____ business.

quiz question 7

Westover never settled back into her community once she left it. She now lives in a flat in _____.

~~~

quiz question 8

Westover was born in a small community in Idaho. The population size was less than _____.

~~~

~ ~ ~

quiz question 9

Westover's parents taught their children wilderness skills and out of religious texts. They even went so far as to have their children prepare getaway bags for when the world would end. Such people are known as _____.

~ ~ ~

quiz question 10

Westover received her undergraduate degree from
_____.

quiz question 11

Westover received her PhD from _____.

~ ~ ~

quiz question 12

Westover was a visiting fellow at _____.

~ ~ ~

Quiz Answers

1.   False
2.   True
3.   Midwifery
4.   Six
5.   History
6.   Junkyard
7.   London
8.   300
9.   Survivalists
10. Brigham Young university
11. Cambridge University
12. Harvard University

Ways to Continue Your Reading

EVERY month, our team runs through a wide selection of books to pick the best titles for readers and reading groups, and promotes these titles to our thousands of readers – sometimes with free downloads, sale dates, and additional brochures.

If you have not yet read the original work or would like to read it again, get the book here.

Want to register yourself or a book group? It's free and takes 1-click.

Register here.

On the Next Page…

Please write us your reviews! Any length would be fine but we'd appreciate hearing you more! We'd be SO grateful.

Till next time,

BookHabits

"Loving Books is Actually a Habit"